flipped eye publishing

The Dishonesty of Dreams

simple words, rendered sublime

The Dishonesty of Dreams
flipped eye publishing
www.flippedeye.net

First Edition
Copyright © Adrienne J. Odasso 2014
Cover Image © iStockphoto.com/Yuri_Arcurs
Cover Design © flipped eye publishing, 2014

All Rights Reserved. No part of this publication may be reproduced, stored in a retrieval system, or transmitted, in any form, or by any means, electronic, mechanical, photocopying, recording or otherwise, without prior consent.

Thanks to the editors of the following publications who published earlier versions of some of the poems in this collection:

The Liberal - *The Word for Love;* **The Dead Mule School of Southern Literature** - *Blue Stars;* **Not One of Us** - *Queen of May;* **Farrago's Wainscot** - *Four Last Things* and *Cold Covers;* **Houston Literary Review** - *Bluff;* **Poetic Diversity** - *Grave Goods;* **Orbis** - *Tomorrow Never Comes Until;* **Thaumatrope** - *Paris, After;* **Sybil's Garage** - *The Hyacinth Girl;* **Dark Mountain** - *Vision;* **Blossombones** - *Five Times I Lived by Water;* **Jabberwocky** - *Cradle Song* and *Dreamer;* **Midnight Echo** - *Five Secret Selves;* **Dreams & Nightmares** - *The Ghosts of Moody Street;* **Cabinet des Fées** - *Cry Wolf;* **Goblin Fruit** - *What They Know;* **Walnut Literary Review** - *Lyuba* and *Touch;* **The Criterion** - *New City;* **Chroma** - *Storms;* **Stone Telling** - *Parallax.*

ISBN: 978-0-9818584-7-0

Editorial work for this book was supported by the Arts Council of England

LOTTERY FUNDED

poems

The Dishonesty of Dreams

Adrienne J. Odasso
2014

Contents

Vision	7
Skin & Paper	8
Parallax	9
Dreamless	10
Pompeii	11
Mantra	12
The Still Point of the Turning World	13
Undertow	15
Lost & Found	17
The Dishonesty of Dreams	18
Hindsight	19
Letters to Lost Friends & Imaginary Lovers	20
Carnal Knowledge	22
Grave Goods	23
Blue Stars	24
Queen of May	25
Bluff	26
Four Last Things	27
Cold Covers	29

The Word for Love	30
Tomorrow Never Comes Until	32
Paris, After	34
At Mortlake	35
Vigil	36
The Hyacinth Girl	37
What They Called Me	38
Five Times I Lived by Water	39
Storms	42
Split Vision	44
The Woman and the Serpent	45
Spell	46
Cradle Song	47
Dreamer	48
Five Secret Selves	50
The Ghosts of Moody Street	52
Monsters	53
Cry Wolf	54
What They Know	55
Lyuba	56
New City	57
Touch	58
Epilogue	59

Vision

Let us begin by saying that the theater burned,
and I was in it. We reached out to many
in terror, newly dead, frantic in passing,
but our hands lanced through them.

I cannot recall where I went, except home
to my kinsmen, who stood in a circle
around the old dining-room table, mourning
as I soundlessly descended the stairs. An anthem

of emptiness bore me, their shining faces rising
to behold what manner of stalking horror
I had become. But they reached up one by one
to touch me as I bound them in one slow circuit

one to another, until I came to my sister,
the youngest, fairest of all. I touched her hands
and gave her all that I had. I transformed then
before her disbelieving eyes, my feathers

the color of iron-blue slate, my seething eyes
silver, pin-pricks of grief. And I told her
in the language of tales that have no ending
that she would be my cherished one

come flood or fire. My soul as a bluebird flew
to the mount of forgetting, where it landed
and stood trembling. The tear-sown path had not
been cleared. Even winged things know fear.

This is a dream of becoming, as all dreams are.

Skin & Paper

In exchange for your marrow, I'll give you
a cloak and the name of this road. Don't expect
to take the right turning at first. There's sorrow
down every single one. Tell me, did you think
that I know not what I'm doing, that these bones
are any but my own? My hair is dyed red
to hide the blood my fingers trail through it.
I slit the ribbon at my throat and dropped the mask
long miles behind us. Are you running
to escape or catch me up? The ties that bind
hold only in slipping. What I love is always just
around the bend. And would you mind much
if I lost the trail on purpose, let the birds find
the bread, chucked the spool that holds the thread
into the river? It's only gold spinning, and starlight
is all we'll ever have. There's no such thing
as the sun, so mark me. Learn it. Cast the dice
as hard as you can at the mirror. Smash it.
Where we're going, you'll have no need
for the sight of skins you've left behind.

Parallax

Black hole at the heart
of Sagittarius: not fish
enough to be Capricorn,
not land-locked enough
to hunt. My paradox
is to be ever at the cusp,
never one / never other,
grasping threads of each.

You called me *boy*,
and I smiled to know
my chimerical self
was untouchable;

you called me *girl*,
and I marveled at how
it is to move between
worlds, ever guessing

what you will say next.

Dreamless

They say we cannot recall details
without flaws, that *Casablanca*
is a classic for what it is not. I hold
shades of your flame in the casement
of my heart, but as for particulars—
they will not stay. In spite of the ire
that I bear you,

there's love here, too.

I look in to make sure that you are sleeping,
hum a web of haunted lullabies: fractured,
flawed enough for beauty.
They'll remember me, and you
through dreamless, half-slitted eyes

will remember, too.

Pompeii

When the feathers close, I'd like to think
that the punishing fire finds you: lovers

locked quiet in one last embrace under rain
and the scorch of flame. I will imagine

my fingers in this clockwork, flicking
dust and gears and misplaced wire aside,

find the place where the words went wrong,
and I will hold you, fierce and inevitable.

Write you still, true, strong.

Mantra

Let me try to explain

that the wind on the water is the voice
in the trees, that the sun on the leaves

is an iron seared to blood, is the reason
for the pain through which I can't breathe.

Let me try to name

my beloved dead for you, spin this thread for you
like the girl locked in the tower that I am:

doomed to stay here, doomed to pray here
in wild, far-ranging voices not my own.

Let me try to say

what I mean; let me repeat
what I have said. Fate

sings in my veins,
and there is hope

in this gold thread.

The Still Point of the Turning World

1. Cather's Run

I thought it was the stream
where the crayfish hid, where the wind
once knocked me clean in. So, I swam
for the bank by way of the deep
and dived instead. The trout teem
in this darkness divisible: my arms
cut a wide, white arc in the shallows
and then down like an arrow,
but bent. I touched rocks six feet under
where my feet slid on algae. Death came
to count the ticking of my fast-held breath.
Shivering, dragged to the surface, I went.

2. Harvard Square

It doesn't work like that, she said.

One does not blink out and rekindle, must not
dare to return to haunt the living. *Well, I dare,*
I said, and the sterling spoon there, tire-bent and slivered

agreed. Some ancient polarity, the universe's heart

hangs on a thread. I bought my fare here, silver, too,
and hung it from a chain. I will not show it to the sun,
nor name it before the living. The prow of this ship

veers star-ward true as traffic lights turn green.

3. Rievaulx Abbey

My breath returned that day
in the rain, up the rise
to where my eyes
fell on the walls. I cried
as if I'd found some hidden answer,
feral comfort
in the lichens' loving scrape.

A chaser of pillars with stories
is what I became:

no hallowed ruin thereafter
was spared my embrace.

4. St. James's Park

Stay with me a while, he says.

And the water rises to the pavement, lifts
my coat, forms the wildest of wings. Sifts
the sand from my skull and gifts me
with snail-shells for teeth. I am

the duck-dive, the bird-cry, the breeze
through the bridges and leaves. I am silence
in the man's startled eyes as I pass by the table
where he sits. Spark recognition. *I'm your ghost,*
I want to say, *and you're mine, but next time—*

Next time won't be so simple:
I'll sink and not rise.

*The eyes beneath which you shiver
will not be mine.*

Undertow

It was as if the storm had known
my slow-eyed waking was long

overdue: the sky stark, swollen
overhead with the knowledge

of my passing from dreams
into death. There are sparrows

caught in the chimney to this
very day, their shallow songs

echoing down the river
of years since I first spoke

of longing to fly. Thunder,
replace this faltering heart

with a clockwork swallow,
give me voice to wonder

at the love of the rain
for the brambles, pin-pricks

leaving my wrists in shambles
as I move between these worlds

that hope to have me. Two clicks
of my heels and I'm gone again,
off on a wing and a prayer,

or maybe

a dare.

Lost & Found

1. Bird Skull

Precious chick, I found you
when I walked waist-high
to morning-glory vines
and couldn't keep my eyes
above ground. There you lay,
fresh as dawn, cast in dew,
less than thought. Drops pooled
where breath once flooded
your beak. I bent and took you
in cupped hands, reverent,
sensing your soft, small spirit
as oh-so-startled it fled.

2. White Shell

So far inland, land-locked, past
the rough touch of forgiving sand
you sat in that self-same high grass,

not far from the shade-covered place
of my hatchling's open grave.
You had a brother, dark, conical,

nothing to your clean, haunting curves.
I took you both home, pretended
that the ghosts of hermit crabs

lived in you. Filled you. Loved.

The Dishonesty of Dreams

I loved you in a dim room—too few,
these moments half-remembered. Your hair
smelled of sassafras, and the air

about us stirred with dust and cotton
adrift from the pillow-slips as we fell
asleep at last upon stiff, slurred sheets.

Then, in the hallowed place where shins
and ankles meet, I brushed your skin
with hesitant fingertips as dawn

rushed me away towards waking.

Hindsight

My first transgression was the absence
of sway in my hips, the way in which
they chose not to spread. My mother pinched
my lips to lend color, spread rose-dust blush
across my cheeks. I never could walk in pumps,
my ankles slender as my father's, and my feet
lacking a sense of propriety: heels careless,
cracked in perpetuity. Now, my doctors say
any seed I may catch will fall fallow, be spat
forth as bitter fruit (and this I know, because
I have twice in great pain birthed only marrow).

Womb turned inside-out, my outsides in
and uncertain of function: what my mother missed,
she pays for in spades. The pill made me retch
till my scrambled coding couldn't bear it.
So late to learn this abundance of flesh
is both more and less than my sum. I am
woman and not. Thirty years gone, this body
is learning still—to live with contradiction.

Letters to Lost Friends & Imaginary Lovers

When I think of you, which is often, snow falls
in the chambers of my heart—not because
we are at war, but because we missed
our one chance to meet. I pause to imagine
the sound of your laughter, and your name
will be the name of my first daughter.

*

In my darkest dreams, I have you:
quick eyes, stark smile. Still, the distance
between longing and having
was always what I wanted:
the harsh, unbelievable thrill
of being the hunted.

*

There is nothing to forgive.

You gave me a boat,
then set me adrift.

And I lived.

*

You hated me for guessing
that it was you—but no, I knew
just who I was looking at
that day beside the fountain.

Under your breath, you swore.
I chattered, spat out cherry-pits,
and loved you all the more.

*

You gave me Eden:

snake in the lilies,
and one last chance

to get even.

*

If I ever lose you, you will
be the hunted, know the thrill
of the chase, be the one whose face
I'll see in rain on the pavement, will throw
my life away when I can't make the call.

*

You will be the one
I've loved enough
to go quietly — that is,
if you'll even dare
to let me go
at all

(& dare you
I shall)

Carnal Knowledge

It's lust for the hard and the cold, the ice-silvered glint of light
through a diamond or a dozen. And as for the gold, I'll have it
any way you can name it: yellow, rose, white. I'm frozen
with fear to admit it, this grit-polished, cloth-finished pleasure
at my throat. No, I can't see it, but I know that your star-struck eyes
will fall there in silence every time you seethe, and every time I breathe
I shiver to know that this fierce and fire-wrought, wire-taut thing
is pure, forged trust. See it and need it. But I forbid you to touch.

Grave Goods

We find a spotted volute not native
to these shores—but, nonetheless,
a needful thing. Small terracotta vases
in the shapes of pomegranates bear paint
in two tones, sport river-ducks tainted
with lead. Also: regard the tumbled stones
shot with veins of crystallized quartz
as signs of sure finesse. And these cups
formed of love and Somerset clay,
you must take them as firm indication
of good taste. This lady did not lay
herself down without thought of the long
years to come, for this stark syndication
of some deity—faceless, throatless—
selflessly held her, drank up her tears.

Blue Stars

What I'd first known of Orion was not so much learned
as felt. I'd lie on my back, small girl in the high summer grass,
and wonder where above the green and sleeping earth
my hunter had gone. And then September's stealthy return
would lead him trailing home before dawn: at this pass
we'd meet, my pale arms blue and tightly folded as I'd ask,
What kept you? With one gallant flash of those true-white eyes
he'd always laugh. No wonder I've never been able to learn
how to trust a man who can't blink. I'd spend my winters
ever after wide awake, searching the sky from cold lakesides
in the snow. I don't know why I took you with me that once
to meet him when he'd edged his closest. He might yet
have fallen for you just as I had, star-struck, lying on my back,
fallen for him. What I'd first known of you was all I'd ever get.

Queen of May

is what you said—and I, scarcely breathing,
said no. I am not what you take me for,

burning and deathless in the sun. I am
no living goddess sent to bless the earth

with love unending. I am helpless
in the grasp of so much grief: this ardor

is my curse on you, letters to the heart
of you: not your Queen of May. Your door

into the vaulted arch of heaven

is dark.

Bluff

Bend with the pain of it, double me down
with the name of it: such vibrant wanting

you've spun from me, strung and held me under
without shame. And I know that you're lying

when I cannot feel the ageless, vein-deep ache
of not belonging, for we are nothing

but what the blackest-played Ace of Spades
has made us. Bright with this stain, dash me down

into drowning: even the stars know better

than to shudder, so thrown

out of orbit.

Four Last Things

1. When You See Her

Sailor, why turn back? What if she's waiting
for her lover long lost, or if she hopes
you'll be the one she comes home to? Straining

your eyes in search of a storm would serve
you better than skinning her, bone and nerve
laid bare for the sea birds to pick. Why veer

from dock and shore, waves and score of years
that she may spend alone? Sailor, be kind

and pay her no mind
when you see her.

2. When You See Me

Close the door, love, and shut your eyes. Try
to see what I am seeing. It's descending
like the dark, only faster, stronger
than life. Being here, stuck between drowning
and dancing, I'm far from where I was
and short of where you are. It's quiet. Why
didn't the lights go out when they wanted?
If we were dying now, who would cover us
with stones, or with wood? Listen, the water is
coming. No more. Close your eyes; shut the door.

3. When You See Us

There is music. There is world enough
and wind on the shallows of the sea
where birds drift. For me, enough

is enough. Just to be in silence is
golden—like the sun, like the fish, like none
of this penance. There is time enough

to know that we are broken, and now this

shows how this

is now.

4. When You Don't

I buy sapphire plums. I drink all night
with the dead. I sing lower than even
you can, and I walk the flooded land
in your stead. When you're gone, left and right

are not. I write until my shaking hands
are still, and the ocean does my will
before the wind's. I speak the seven
names of an unknown god. Your eyes fill

the shallows. I see you.

Go home now.

Cold Covers

Behind the cobbled walls rise linden
and bramble, where the low grass was home
to kings' soldiers. So, too, the young lovers
stole in secret through the branches, basking

in the noon sun's splintered gold. *Dear prince,*
he said, sweet prince. *They'll scale the shadows*
and find us here by sunset. No laughter
can change this chance; no breath under blue

of the brilliant twilight will find them
alive. *Listen,* he said, *now listen*
to the leaves and watch the lichen
glisten, my sweet prince and true.

They're sleeping, so cover the low grass
with stone. Linden, bramble and rue.

The Word for Love

For Rumi and Shams, wherever they wander.

1. The Word for Love

The word for love was not *love*,
or even *kiss*. It was bliss
beyond the dust of the road
on which you met him, blinded

by the last rose-shaded flames
of sunset. Let the desert stones
that will in time shape his death
be your comfort; find the place

where the ones who know the words
for *touch* and *wine* and even *God*
have hidden themselves from the face

of hate, and there
partake of *grace*.

2. Tabrizi

I see you now, dear wanton. On your back
you pray, begging, sand-scoured lips athirst
for verse. You rode in, dark stranger, wrecked
the poet's books; I never knew. What I saw
came much later, trysts and your death. Now,
there is this weaving: a shadowed room above
in the eaves of the inn where he led you, laid
you down upon silk-shot wool, birds and trees
knotted fierce as your breath. Your fingers caught
in scattered fringe, pulled taut as your hips to his.

3. Dervish

It is what love will do, what it demands
of fools who fall. Meet insult with miracle,
miracle with wonder: you will wax dumb
with the weight of his stare. And much later
you will sink, sink and spin, spin and curse
the day you were thus blessed. This night is
for the moment what you want, but by dawn
all of Konya will talk; their great teacher, this
lawyer lost, is a lover of men. Just for now
your voice is silent, your whirling heart his.

4. No Words

And there is no word for *loss*
or for *tears*, no balm for *pulse
stopped in its tracks*, no wish
to halt your screaming—*Shams,*

come back! No sigh for *grave
I can't visit by daylight*, no voice
left in the void. You'd drown
your books if it would save him

from scorching sand. *Touch*
and *wine* and *God* and *love*
were his. There is no word

for comfort, no word

for *this*.

Tomorrow Never Comes Until

1.

The night before we left, I rearranged the dust:
swept it into new corners, left it in rifts

to die. And although good at planning trips,
I'm persistently amidst the forgotten mourners

of the one twist of fate we always fail to trust.

2.

I had to send away for the one seashell
I'd always wanted—so rare that it cost
a small fortune, but this tale ends as well
as it must. Salt in lieu of what I've lost.

3.

The morning I left, I scraped all the rust
off the doorknobs, canceled my options

on those dumb jobs. What is there for me if
nothing will come to me now? I'm drifting

away from your shore. Just stay or be gone.

4.

I had to send away
for a skin-thick sail
to patch my wings.

Paris, After

With nothing left but the Seine,
we'd rebuild the isles
slowly, one by one.

From the ruins of Notre Dame,
a library of songs
set in stone.

At Mortlake

Witch-wood, sage. Amaranth. The answer
is not in the glass or in the flame,

but in his breath. Sing on, choirs eclipsed
by wanting, until the candle gutters

with the shudder of his frame before
the scry. Hands entwining slither

past belt and folds of wool, snarl in the spool
so long left still. Fingers curl to fill it—

warp weft *sigh*. Work the shuttle, wet his thigh.

Vigil

After Sappho

Sweetbitter unmanageable creature
who steals in after nights spent dancing,
wild-haired until sunrise—where have you been?

There is no particular rapture
for me to find quietly waiting
in this ash-strewn bed. If you had seen

me this evening, patient and alone,
you would have wondered why my dreaming
eyes have grown so starkly shadowed.

Sweetbitter unmanageable creature
who steals in when I least expect
these cold sheets to part, I'll ask you again—

where, my wayward and wild-haired love

have you been?

The Hyacinth Girl

Forget fear in a handful of dust,
forget your shadow at evening rising
to meet you. If it's fear that you want,
I'll show you fear that slips in, surreptitious,
while you're sleeping. I'll show you trust
that betrays your every unconscious breath,
threads terrors through your heart unsuspecting
of death. And the shades you will face there can't
be held accountable for what will rise around us
in the gloom: no blossoms, no scent of royal purple
will bloom for you here. No laughter will lead you,
blinking, back into daylight, for in dreaming
you have crossed the river of all regrets
for good. Girl, leave your flowers behind you.

What They Called Me

Forgive me, purples, for I have penned
nothing since June, demanded too soon
that love descend undeserved. That grace
give restitution for harm perceived
without sight. That the salt-tracked mask
of my face be gilt-washed, my sand-filled
eyes stilled with diamonds. I am grieved
with absence even now, even knowing how
I could not have ever hoped to hold
such precious weeds: these hyacinths bleeding
sunlight in my unsuspecting hands.

Five Times I Lived by Water

1. Cuyahoga

My father claims that the river caught fire
on the night I was born. My research suggests
that he is either lying or misremembers
and has conflated the strange event
with my slow coming. Whenever I ask
my mother, she says that I burned
worse than any brand on my sluggish way
into artificial light. I wonder
if the truth lies somewhere in between:
that the river caught fire at the hint
of my arrival, lent my eyes its gleam.

2. North Fork

Too slight to be a river, yet too large
to seem a creek. My grandfather led me
close by the water, explained the trick
of keeping firm footing out in the deep.
I proved a fast fisher of monsters
inside the first hour. One after another,
sunfish and trout, speckled catfish and chubs
foundered hungry on my hooks. We'd keep
only the ones deemed best for eating.
As for the rest, they'd earned their living,
having taught me how weakness looks.

3. Charles

At least this place, too, has blue herons
and kingfishers that dive from shopping cart
to weed-bed, from bicycle part to pier
before rising again. I'll stay with you
here in this soft, polluted silence till
all the city sinks and water rises
past our door. After that, I'm uncertain
of where I will go. The ocean is far
from us, but nearer than it was when first
I came. Before I leave, I'll have one last
boon to ask, and it's this: return my name.

4. Ouse

I could hate this country for giving me
something to love—spired, frigid ruins
that fit my mind's frail landscape like a glove.
I'm told that her dear cousin, Mother Thames,
yields up pipe-stems and pots, even bodies
belonging to souls that London forgot.
For now, I'm where I am, biding my time
until our own tame river turns to flood,
swallows the high turrets' stones, even burns
my too-long dulled eyes with brightest blood.

5. Aire

I'm telling my father that the river
has turned to ice overnight, become
a landing hazard to every gull
within a twenty-mile radius.
If I could only see her smile, I'd tell
my mother what it looks like when they slide
in a blur of dull feathers. This is us,
my grandfather and me, separated
by fish-killing distance. My heart is full
as the ocean that bore me, or the hull
of this steamship, ablaze with remembrance.

Storms

There was that time on Earth, when snow
fell on us like antique prayers from the mountain
where a bead-addled hermit lived. The stones
we climbed to the courtyard were ancient,
locked in ice and grit, but would fall
from grace no sooner than spring had lit.

You had wondered if your language
would ever survive in that frigid clime.
I had said I was afraid that clicks,
hums, and sighs might sink deep in the drifts.

There was that time in the guts of the ship,
when sparks pelted us, an unforgiving rain
upon our bare skin. We were heedless
of broken gears and an engine stretched far
beyond its years. Your feather-swift fingers
spoke of wanting, an inscrutable thing
that you had professed not to know.

I had pondered our strange marriage,
a marvel of silence unshattered
even now. You had hissed for me
to keep quiet. And then, we'd kissed.

That time on the surface. Somewhere. Chaos
unwinding in gusts of flame and steam,
a worldscape too unstable to hold
your luminescence. Still, we escaped
with our tendrils and packs entangled, backs
scraped raw by the roaring cold.

You had told me this: that for you, love
held no form but my frailty. A human face.
All of my heart in one hailstorm. Breath.

Peace.

Split Vision

Turn the tables or the corner. Smoke rises
from my upturned hands and stings my eyes

with this beginning, for I cannot learn
from what was. So I will chase them through

the Shadows of the Valley of Death, these lies
resembling love, and then I will find them

though all Hell should rise to meet me
in the trying. Read in these pages the blue

of the evening. I have left it behind me,
and the stars be my diamonds now, distant

cold pulses of flame in an instant
unwinding—

and the tables *burned*.

The Woman and the Serpent

I prize the taste of this rare fruit
above the sting of carnal knowledge:

the tang
of these teeth
as they pierce, then sink
like lodestone
in the deep.

I learned to breathe underwater
for the sake of our joining. I wonder,

do serpents
take their lovers
home for tea?

Since to live I must pass this poison
on to another—or so I gather—

there will never be
a home here
for me.

Spell

After Sappho

Gold anklebone cups, dip low
and fill as she dances. Be still
as the buried, then grow quick
with the current on which
you're carried. Bear her close
by the bank-side, where the brook
slows enough to bless the sand
with gifts from below, then lay her
to rest. I'll drink from the curve
of her foot, dip to kiss her hand.

Cradle Song

Sink it just above the breastbone. *There*. You'll crack the ribs
much faster than if you hit the belly first. See where

the scar started, and note when it ends. This wound's ancient,
but you'll open it soon again and sure enough. These entrails

speak volumes in signs and omens: one tendril is sufficient
to tell you how this ageless story's gone. It's in the blood

and bone that the deepest love lies hidden. Please don't shy
from this, carcass and cradle. It'll hold you now. There, *there*.

Dreamer

Imagine: nightly, there's the shift of breath from waking into sleep
that's like crossing the Blackwater barefoot—ankles, knees, hips
submerged in the murk of a slumber that finds you so reluctant
that it must tie weights to your slim, steel-strong wrists
and drag you under. You were never meant to reach the other side—

*

where the sky's brushed over with high, threatening cirrus. Meanwhile,
the fire pit a mile off is burning out with morning's first birds
alight in the sapling birches, which you tugged free, roots screaming
revenge, and sank them from wide, sailing arcs into the backs of boys
who hated you for your unfailing defiance. You can bet on it—

*

because you have visited this horror time and again, the hesitant brush
of pitying fingers at the backs of your hands as you pass, bleeding
   blindly
from the gut as you climb upward still, while beneath, the sightless
   tower keeling
tells your weary knees that your strength is insufficient. You will fail
before you reach the apex. Against the falling, you'll rail. And cling—

*

to keep the floor from spinning. Awake again, in a place that knows no
   time
but plenty of space. Still dying. Did you think you'd cheated in trying
to reach those scimitar clouds? This isn't Babel. This is your passing
   wish:

in knowing his lover's kiss, perhaps, you'll carry it into your own dark
    waking
away from a place you'll fix firmly in time out of mind, non-existent. As
    for space—

*

it's small, cramped. You've been in this tunnel for hours, hands and
    knees scoured
of skin, but still you'll crawl ever forward towards an ending that's not
    yours
but that you'd die for. It's knowing that you are not and have never
    been the self
you were born into. It's knowing that your frail wrists and hands, your
    skinned fours
were made for telling others' stories. The water recedes, delves deep.
    You can't help—

*

wishing,
dreamer, that you were still
asleep.

Five Secret Selves

1. Inanna

I'm nobody's mother and certainly
nobody's fool. My father's daughter
to the death, I'll chase you down back-streets

and hope for the best. This red lipstick?
Do you like it? Took ages to find.

My highest heels don't match it, but my eyes
don't mind. Come out and have a smoke, won't you,
my love? I've only got a few left.

(Ten thousand kisses, all of them my best.)

2. Sefret

I tried to
stop the bleeding, but the flow
wouldn't staunch; not even the Nile at high tide
could drown it. I'd show you what I lost, but the river swept it away
before I could say goodbye. It's back to the temple with me, farewell to
    my pride
and the child they'd have never let me keep. The swells are deep
with forgetting where I lingered. Those still, tiny fingers
won't ever find the shallows. Come tomorrow,
I'll lie on cool sandstone and sing
until morning, and then
I will go.

3. Åsta

I left my knife
in its sheath. No reason

to bother when he's not
coming home. I'd stay here

till dawn, but my daughter
will not want to return

to the longhouse

alone.

4. Marianne

Revolution's not kind. Don't ever believe it.
They'll steal your ring and leave you for dead

if you risk it. Always learn to shoot.
You never know when hitting the broad side

of a barn will not be enough. Always yearn
for something better than men who only know

how to die.

5. Uriel

I have said to you all of the secret things
that I have ever meant to say. I will find you in the end
and bring you home. Beloved, I saw you in the door

and I will be the one to see you gone.

The Ghosts of Moody Street

The closest thing that we have to shipwrecks
on this stretch of the Charles are sunken
shopping carts. Ducks and kingfishers perch
on the handlebars, squabbling for rights
to poach each swanky fish condominium.

From the bridge, I can see that somebody
has razed the great milkweed forest
ere the monarchs have had the chance to hatch;
What I call unfairness, the rest of this town
might call maintenance or necessity.

Down on the dock that isn't a dock,
Charon has set up a business
for himself with a tiny red boat
and a sign advertising scenic tours
for fifteen dollars. I would take the trip
out of curiosity, but my fare
is hanging about my neck right where

he can see that I believe
he still exists.

Monsters

I know the day I'd choose, right down to
the hour, which I tell by the way the sun

bares its teeth in the dust-moted dusk.
This city begins even when we're done,

a place for the meanest kind of trusting
and loving in. Still, you didn't take me:

even when I was sure that I'd got you,
window-glass blurred your guile. I'm dying

of poison, slowly—and you, Medusa in
reflection, did you even chance to see

my terrified smile?

Cry Wolf

After Marie de France, "Bisclavret"

What that uppity Norman bitch will never tell you
is that he stank to high heaven just home from the hunt,
left muddy footprints on the painted tiles of my parlor,
and drank till the cider was gone. What was I to do
but trap him, see to it that the brute lost his armor
in favor of claws? Even my father's hawking mutts
knew better than to dribble on the floor. Small wonder
the King took him in, for one animal will always
know another—and heaven help him if it had been
the Queen who'd got savaged instead! What would the court
have said, what when his noseless firstborn daughter made
her first mask? And what of my own daughters, joyless,
deprived of the green scent of spring, of summer flowers
I knew once, but that they can never guess? Just for sport,
Highness, I wish you'd hunted him, chased him senseless
before the kill. I wonder if he'd have changed then, but now

he never will.

What They Know

An uneasy ghazal

The world thinks me a villain, but what do they know?
True, their children are missing. Oh, yes, they *know*.

Have Alice's parents thought to check the rabbit-hole?
Might have been that careless gardener, for all they know.

And what of Wendy and her pack of little brothers?
Window-washers are guilty, leave latches undone. *They* know.

Even Little Red's jaunt in the woods is suspect:
Mum and Dad just sent her off, secure in what they know.

Can a mother show her daughter the path to Paradise,
where perilous creatures will teach her all that they know?

Can a father force open his son's wayward eyes
to realms of horrors that will show him what they know?

Adventures are needful things, easiest to miss
when blinded by cheats and comforts—what they know.

And at the heart of my tale, the root of all evil, is this:
the trick to what they know, Child, is what they don't. *You* know.

Lyuba

Little girl, you are loved
beyond reason, although death
should bar your knowing. What season
saw you to your grave? What breath
frozen deep in the cave of your chest
will tell us what frail flowers
you grazed? When they cut your cheek,
I felt shame, wished I could save
your teeth from the furrowed brows
of men with scalpels. What woman
could have healed you, kept you safe
from the others? Did they know
you were loved once before
by your bereaved mother?
I imagine her over you,
helpless to do anything
but mourn.

New City

I've spent some time in this quiet afterlife
dreaming journeys just beyond my reach.
The men by the waterside watch me
as I study them, lift their eyes to seek
my knees as I flick ash against the sky.
There is nothing here that I could want
more than wishing for this silence. I'll teach
my mind to be still, my thoughts to swim
below in the breezes skimming askance
the brook. My stillborn poems will haunt
this small and squared space long after
I'm gone. I turn from my watch alone
to close the latch, desiring little else
than plum-skin and smoke
between my teeth.

Touch

You have scattered sharp pieces of yourself
across this wide world for me to find,
errant pieces of a cypher in which I have no help
save for the mockery of your leaving. As for the notes
you send from out of the ether, I wouldn't mind
if you'd be more specific. A poem, a caper,
a jest: this is what I am to you, the rest
of a story you'd rather not finish. Unwind
yourself before me one last time in the hush
of morning. I can't sleep for the sound of your breath.

Epilogue

*in my dream, we could not find
the ruins reputedly near
to the inn; my mother*

*argued that a rumor is less
than a fib, but I knew better*

*that the hull of the hill held wonders
hid since time out of mind, that the wind
would guide me if I raced*

*from casement to door,
from stairwell to floor*

*and the woods
oh the woods, I cannot tell you
they were still as if winter*

*had not fled my much-wronged love
and even if I do not like it*

*I want to know the mind
that made this shelter
of ivory, of bone not*

remembered

Thank you for buying **The Dishonesty of Dreams**. Adrienne J. Odasso is a fabulous poet, editor and owner of an overabundance of books, tea, and aquarium fish. You can follow her work and projects online at:
LiveJournal: http://ajodasso.livejournal.com
Twitter: http://twitter.com/ajodasso

—§—

flipped eye publishing is dedicated to publishing powerful new voices in affordable volumes. Founded in 2001, we have won awards and international recognition through our focus on publishing fiction and poetry that is clear and true, rather than exhibitionist.

If you would like more information about flipped eye publishing, please join our mailing list online at **www.flippedeye.net**.

www.ingramcontent.com/pod-product-compliance
Lightning Source LLC
Chambersburg PA
CBHW051703040426
42446CB00009B/1280